DISCOVERING MY EXPERIENCE OF GOD:

Awareness and Witness

Frank DeSiano, CSP and Kenneth Boyack, CSP

PAULIST PRESS
New York
Mahwah, New Jersey

ISBN: 0-8091-3300-8

Published by Paulist Press
997 Macarthur Boulevard
Mahwah, New Jersey 07430

Printed and bound in the
United States of America

CONTENTS

DISCOVERING MY EXPERIENCE OF GOD is dedicated to Rev. Alvin A. Illig, CSP, the pioneer Paulist missionary and evangelist, who contributed greatly to the advent of Catholic evangelization in the United States.

ACKNOWLEDGEMENTS

We are grateful, first of all, to the Paulist community of which we are members. The Paulists have encouraged us to explore new areas of evangelization and contemporary religious awareness, and this book is one product of that exploration.

We are grateful for the hundreds of people who participated in the Paulist Evangelization Training Institute which we have been co-directing for several summers. Their eagerness for evangelization and their willingness to be part of the early development of this exercise made this book possible.

We are grateful to those who helped with the final reading of this manuscript and gave many valuable suggestions: Sr. Rose Marie Henschke, DC, Mr. Neil Parent, Ms. Kathy Schwartz, Sr. Susan Wolf, SND, Rev. Lawrence Connolly, CSP, and Mrs. Monica Theis Huber.

We are, finally, grateful to the leadership that Fr. Alvin Illig, CSP, gave to the Paulist community and the American church. His pioneering work and enthusiasm were both a support and challenge for us.

Part I

The Exercise

A PERSONAL INVITATION

This spiritual exercise—*Discovering My Experience of God*—is about you, your life and your experiences. Through this exercise you will be guided through a set of reflections that can help you put into words what we, as Americans and Catholics, often have such a difficult time saying: what our experience of God is.

We invite you to an exercise that will open your spirit, prod your memories, evoke different feelings, and help you begin to develop a vocabulary about your religious experience that is authentically yours.

We all have images of what "religious language" is like—maybe sermons, or pious books, or the language that is used on religious talk shows. Yet no rule stipulates that religious language has to be a certain way or that our religious experiences have to come in a certain package.

Discovering My Experience of God is an invitation for you to discover, through memory and writing, the ways that God has touched your life through *your* own personal history. Can we look back at our lives and see patterns, events, threads and intuitions that have composed our religious story? Brought us to a consciousness of God? Shaped our spirituality? Formed our faith?

We believe that the more people understand their own religious experience, the more they can affirm God's presence in their lives. And the more people can affirm God's presence in their lives, the freer they can be to share that experience with others.

Discovering My Experience of God, then, does not stop with introspection and reflection; it leads, rather, to a greater awareness of God in daily life, to a greater ability to describe that awareness, and to a greater freedom to share that with others when appropriate.

3

Thank you for taking the time to open yourself before God and to try to discover, in words and memory, your experience of God.

HOW TO USE THIS BOOK

If You Are Using This Book by Yourself . . .

Discovering My Experience of God provides a ready opportunity to reflect on your personal faith in the privacy of your home. Consider this a mini-retreat experience and expect that the Holy Spirit will reveal the rich contours of your faith as you do this exercise. As you proceed, read Chapter 1 first and then complete the exercise which is in Chapter 2. Once finished, you will want to read Chapters 3 and 4 in Part II which will help you to reflect on what you have written.

If You Are Using *Discovering My Experience of God* as Part of a Group . . .

You may be using this book as part of a retreat or as part of a workshop. In either case, you will be doing the exercises as part of a community of people who not only want to discover the elements of their own faith journey but also want to become better equipped and more confident to share their faith with others.

Your leader will help your group get oriented to what he or she wants to accomplish and the ways in which *Discovering My Experience of God* will help the group to attain its goals. When you finish the day, or the two evenings, be sure to read Chapters 1, 3 and 4. You will benefit greatly from spending this additional time reflecting on your own experience in relation to the group.

If You Are Leading a Group . . .

Those having the opportunity to lead others through *Discovering My Experience of God* will be able to provide a great service. We know that the large majority who use and evaluate this instrument rate it in the "very good" to "excellent" range. Consequently, you can have great confidence that what you are presenting to people will be well received.

As you prepare to use this instrument as part of your retreat or workshop, be sure to complete Chapters 1 and 2 yourself, if you haven't done so already. Chapter 2 contains important information about the various parts of this exercise and what they are probing. Unless you have gone through the chapters, you can hardly introduce them to others. Chapters 3 and 4 will provide you with important considerations to help others as they do this exercise—from a personal and a theological perspective. Meanwhile, Chapter 5, "Tips for Those Administering the Instrument," provides information and examples which will enable you to administer this instrument with competence and confidence.

1. YOUR EXPERIENCE AND GOD

Experience.

Can any word be harder to define or any idea more elusive? Yet it is the one undeniable factor in every human life. Because we are conscious, loving, connected human beings, we all have experience.

Our experience sweeps back to our earliest memories, vague or sharp images of people who shaped our lives, moments of incredible consolation and events of sudden terror. It touches all the stages we use to define our existence—pre-adolescence, teenage years, early adulthood, middle age and senior citizen— even though we cannot say for sure how we passed from one stage to another. No stage was clearly marked for us.

Experience covers our most private moments—dreamless nights of thought, musings over a journal, inner conversations on our way to work, intense moments of prayer. And experience also concerns our most connected moments—days of family gatherings, first moments of love, being embraced by parents or embracing our own children and the bustle of daily work, with its dozens of tasks to be accomplished, people to see, and deadlines to meet. Indeed, we experience as individuals, as members of families, as friends, as residents of a city, as citizens, as members of one species dwelling on one of many planets in unlimited space.

EXPERIENCE AND STORY

Isn't it true that our days have a uniformness to them? We rise, wash, eat, work or do our tasks, eat dinner and then rest and sleep. These generally predictable events form something like a background rhythm to our life, episodes and happenings that occur in sequence, day by day, year by year.

Yet these daily happenings, which constitute the elements of a life, are not what we first think of when we try to recall our experience or describe our experience to another. From these episodes of daily life we cull impressions, conclusions, images and perhaps even a philosophy that we more readily call our experience. We don't talk, for example, about class every morning at 9:00 in the fifth grade; rather, we talk about our childhood, what school was like or what it was like to grow up. Everyone has experience, then, but not all of us can point to it with equal ease. We hear children trying to tell a story that is too long for them, starting over, interrupting themselves, troubling themselves to get one image right. Poets, on the other hand, seem to be able to compress whole fabrics of experience into simple and profound images which open up a picture of life. Wise older people can sum up the meaning of a generation with one or two phrases. Parents begin to grasp the meaning of their own adolescence by the episodes they see in their children.

The two together—the daily episodes and the larger story we form—make up the experience of our lives, that background which is so decisive for everything we do. Out of that background we reflect on our past, find energy for the present moment and prepare ourselves for experiences yet to come. Out of that background we make conclusions about people we've known and bring these conclusions to our meetings of new people. This background allows others to describe us one way or another: we are optimists, doubters, survivors, sinners or saints.

We are each of us, then, forming stories, culling our daily happenings in such a way that the meaning of our lives emerges. Indeed, from this process, we ourselves emerge.

GOD AND OUR EXPERIENCE
Just as stories give us larger pictures of the meaning of the individual episodes of our life, so our religious story gives us a religious picture of that same life.

If life is given to us, moment by moment, isn't it a gift from God? If the events of my life open before me, within me and through me, am I not a participant in the life God is forming for me?

Yet our common cultural prejudice, a by-product of an overly flat modern vision, is that God is not part of our everyday experience. Rather, God is seen to be experienced separately, unusually and, therefore, rarely. We often have this assumption, and we maintain it in spite of all the evidence of our experience. For we do have religious experience—episodes of reflection, prayer, hope, intuition, decision, doubt, joy and even ecstasy—along with all the other events of our life. And these experiences, while coloring those other events, are not separated from them. We can even understand our religious experience as a dimension of life in both its ordinariness and its unusualness.

The serious illness of a parent, for example, is certainly a medical episode, dotted with the data of X-rays, tests, charts and consultations; and it is certainly a family event, with all the evocations of what our parents have done for us, our sense of obligation and helplessness, and our feelings that the foundations of our lives are being shaken. But it is also a religious experience, a time when we try to comprehend what it means to live, to be given life, and for life to come to an end. Indeed, we cannot know what hope, need, dependence, anticipation and love are all about without life's opportunities and trauma. Religion comes packed into it.

Acknowledging my experience of God is acknowledging that God has been part of my life, through its various episodes and phases, through its trials and triumphs. It is a way of saying that God is also part of our stories.

DISCOVERING OUR EXPERIENCE

Why, then, do we have to *discover* our religious experience? If experience is the stuff of life, if everyone has experience, if God is part of that experience, isn't it all rather clear, transparent, obvious?

Unfortunately, no.

We are, first of all, far more likely to attribute religious experience to others than to ourselves. We perhaps imagine that others pray more forthrightly, live lives with greater moral clarity,

9

sense a divine presence and get inspired by the Holy Spirit far more than we do. Like so many other areas of life, we sometimes discount our own gifts and experience because we prefer to be dazzled by what we imagine others have.

Additionally, we've been disposed to think of religious experience as something unusual. Countless stories of saints in ecstasy and images of people tossing canes aside in miraculous healings have conditioned us to think of religion as some kind of supernatural energy that snaps our attention, zaps our experience and leaves us enraptured. But consider the moments of silent prayer, the experiences of years of worship, the hearing of hundreds of scriptural passages, the simple religious sharing we have done with so many as part of our daily life. We often discount these, even though they are exactly the kinds of things that shape our religious lives.

Also, even should we begin to acknowledge our religious experience, we have not formed comfortable and natural ways to express our faith. Whether it is our American sense that religion is private, or the kind of overly individual piety in which many of us were formed, or simply a natural kind of bashfulness, the truth is that we are often speechless when it comes to talking about our own experience of God, of faith, of religion.

For this reason, we offer this spiritual exercise as a "discovery" of our experience of God, as a way to bring together loose impressions and inarticulate senses into something like a story, our story, the story of our personal faith. This discovery is a way of accessing our experiences so that they can be acknowledged, appreciated and perhaps shared.

EXPERIENCE AND DISCIPLESHIP

One of the dangers of talking about experience is that, by definition, it is cast in personal terms. Experience, we feel, is personal to each one of us. No one can take my experience away; it is part of me.

Yet the more we think that way, the harder it is for us to consider sharing the experience of others. If faith is so intensely personal and individual, can one person ever enter the experiences of another? We often hear today people saying, "You wouldn't understand; it's not your 'thing.' "

The scriptures, particularly the gospels of Jesus, help to correct this overly personal sense of experience. For we can understand the gospels precisely as the recounting of those who experienced Jesus and the experiences of the early communities of those who came to believe in Jesus. Certainly these encounters were personal. But they were also social, communal. People gathered to share and celebrate the experiences they had and, through worship, continued to reflect on and develop their faith.

The experience of the disciples compelled them to share this good news. They did not proclaim some rarefied event that only a very few chosen ones could attain. Rather, they witnessed in order to create points of access for people so they could be touched, changed and saved by a new life in Christ. The gospel stories still have the power to envelop us even today, in our parishes and in our easy chairs, in the experience of Jesus. When the paralyzed man lies before Jesus, we lie there too (Mk 2:1–12). When the woman crawls into Simon's house in repentance, we are inching along with her (Lk 7:36–50). When the crowds hear the beatitudes of Jesus, we hear them too (Mt 5:1–12).

Paul's letters to ancient cities are letters to our own communities and families. Luke's account of the growth of the early church gives account to our own church experience. John's meditations on love's meaning and Paul's hymn to love make us want to live for love ourselves.

To get clear about our own experience does not lock us up in some introspective cocoon where we sink more deeply into ourselves. On the contrary, getting clear about our own experience helps us make that experience accessible to others—so others may hear what we have heard, see what we have seen, know what we have come to know.

Every one of us who has been privileged to experience God through Jesus is called, by that very experience, to discipleship, to witness, to have our experience open possibilities for other people. Isn't that what happened to us? Haven't we entered a life of faith because others were willing to share their experience with us?

Imagine what it would be like if each of us felt confident and competent to share faith when the occasion presents itself. We live next door to inactive Catholics, to people who are searching for God, to people who are looking for words of strength in times of personal crisis or sadness. What if we Catholics could respond to these situations with a sensitive and appropriate sharing of our faith experience?

Imagine, too, all the work situations in which we find ourselves: building construction, computer sales, factory assembly. What would it be like if each of us in these work situations felt confident and competent to share our personal faith experience? We are not talking, of course, about pounding people over the head with scripture quotes or attacking them with pre-packaged methods of proselytizing. Not at all. Rather, we are talking about understanding the contours of our own journeys of faith and, because of that understanding, feeling comfortable to share that gift with others.

Think, too, of our families. How awkward many of us are about expressing anything truly serious with our family members! What would it be like if husbands and wives felt comfortable in sharing their faith experience with each other, and with their friends and relatives? And when children come along, what would it be like if parents not only could pass on the marvelous truths of their Catholic religion but also could share a personal witness with their children? Wouldn't that strengthen family life? Wouldn't that make the faith of families grow stronger?

Discovering My Experience of God is designed to facilitate religious awareness and sharing. Through this simple but powerful pastoral tool, we want to help in the process of equipping Catholics to acknowledge their own religious experience and to feel more comfortable in sharing that with others.

If you would like to become better acquainted with the elements of your own religious story, if you would like to find words to say what God has come to mean to you, if you would like to acknowledge the ways in which faith has come to be so important for you through others, we invite you to take time to complete the exercise in Chapter 2. Go through this chapter prayerfully, reflectively, expectantly. And, seeing God's presence in your life, maybe it will help you to make God's presence known in the lives of others.

2. COMPLETING "DISCOVERING MY EXPERIENCE OF GOD"

This exercise comes in two parts: a worksheet found on pages 21 to 29 and a summary sheet found on pages 30 to 34. Take a moment to review these pages. These two components of the exercise go hand in hand. First, using a pen or pencil, you will complete the worksheet. Feel free to scratch, ramble, erase, muse, doodle, or do whatever you want while you are gathering your memories and associations. Most people spend about an hour covering the eight areas; you may spend more or less time.

Next, you will complete the summary sheet, which will take you about a half hour. This part of the exercise enables you to put your initial scratchings into a certain order and calls for rewriting and editing in order to form a coherent story. One note of caution here. If you find yourself resisting the outline offered on the summary sheet, try to stay with it. This part helps you to put your experiences into a less private and more accessible form. Further, it will enable you to see that your faith experience is not meant to be kept only for yourself, but can be a tremendous source of grace for others.

Before you begin, we invite you to read about each area of this exercise which we explain in the next section and then to complete the exercise itself. When you have finished, you will want to look at Chapter 3 which will provide some immediate considerations about the exercise.

THE AREAS
Discovering My Experience of God asks a person to look at his or her experience through the eyeglass of eight areas. Each area probes specific memories, interests and associations. These areas, once exposed, get bundled into a coherent story. When you go through this exercise, you may find different and deeper aspects of your story.

This section presents these different areas to help clarify what kind of memories or associations are being sought and why.

AREA 1. THE BACKDROP

As you reflect on your life, what are the most important religious dates that you remember? Think about your confirmation, marriage, ordination, religious profession, or other events. On the timeline below, place those dates and events on the top of the line and then, below the line, jot down the key people associated with that experience. These dates form the context for your personal witness.

Background Information

This part of the exercise asks you to draw a "time line" of the significant religious events in your life. It also asks you to recall the people associated with those events. The dates, events and people are placed along the line from left to right, with the earlier ones coming first. The dates and events go on top of the line, while the people associated with them go on the bottom. Figure 1 gives an example.

Figure 1

1934	1945	1952	1979	1986
First Communion	Marriage	Son born	Dad dies	Retreat

. . . .

Mom	Fr. Jim	Eddie	Mom	Fr. Jim
Aunt	Bill			
Julie				

This information helps you form a general framework that includes people and events, as well as related images and memories that influenced your spiritual journey. You can see, perhaps, some growth or change over a lifetime, or you may see that the names of some people come up over and over again.

AREA 2. FIRST AWARENESS
Try to remember when you first experienced an awareness of God. Recall the setting, the people present, the particular feelings, how old you were. Write these memories below. Also reflect on whether or not this awareness persisted.

Background Information
This area helps you focus on the times in your life when God was seen as *real*. The exercise is not looking here for thunder-and-lightning revelations, but rather the point when you said to yourself, "Well, maybe there is a God after all." Or "I am starting to find myself concerned about God in my relationships to others."

You may be tempted to think of this in terms of an exceptional experience, but resist that temptation. If faith were dependent on thunder-and-lightning types of revelations, few would be believers.

AREA 3. POWERFUL MOMENTS
Recall the most powerful religious moments in your life—times of great feeling, awakening, or decisive events. (These can be times of joy as well as sorrow.) What happened? What were your feelings? What images of God did they give you? What images of other people?

Background Information
This area, in contrast to the previous one, *is* looking for powerful experiences—as you define them. A powerful experience for one person may be insignificant in the life of another. You should have no presumptions about the packages in which religious experiences come nor about what makes for a powerful religious moment. You are your own judge of that!

Writing this information helps you to recall that such spiritual experiences have actually happened in your own life, even though you may not allude to them very often.

AREA 4. IMAGES OF GOD

Describe the predominant images of God in your life right now. Is God a strong father, a consoling mother, a healer, a savior, a providential guide, a . . . ?

Background Information

Discovering My Experience of God invites you at this point to recall images of God. The reason is to help you see connections between your own experience and your personal "theology," that is, your personal way of making sense of God through images.

Every person must have something in mind when the word "God" is said, and that something must be an image. True, that image may be more or less conceptualized, but there must be some *image* because that is the way the human mind works.

You might begin to reflect on the patterns of your experiences and how these affect the symbolic images of God you have formed. If you have been through many difficulties in life, God may be more readily "imagined" as a support or even as an avenger. If your life has seemed filled with opportunities and with little stress, God may be perceived as a generous parent. Our life patterns affect our image of God.

Perhaps this exercise can be a way for you to begin "reimagining" God through recalling your experience and its patterns.

AREA 5. CHANGE

Look back on your life and identify your greatest change. It may have been during your teen or young adult years, or at the beginning or later points of your marriage, or at the start of a career or vocation. As you think about this change, recall what life was like for you "before" and "after." The areas below will help you to reflect on this experience.

My greatest change:

The ways I perceive myself "before" and "after":

　　　Before　　　　　　　　　　After

What was the role of faith in that change?

Who helped you most during that change? And what was their faith?

Background Information

This area addresses the issue of change. If Christianity is based on God's revelation and our response, and our response involves conversion and change, this area asks what kinds of changes we have experienced.

Perhaps you will think: "I haven't experienced any change." But that would mean that you haven't lived! We have experienced change; believing people, responding to God's love, do undergo conversion.

If we can begin to reflect on the changes in our lives, we may begin to see our conversion story revealed. It may be a story of moving from selfishness to generosity, from insecurity to confidence, from shyness to openness, from doubt to faith. It may be a story of intellectual questioning and quest, satisfied only in the mystery of God. Sometimes it may be a story of brokenness and desperation in which one was rescued by what could only be divine help.

It is also important to see how the presence of others has been a factor in the changes of our lives. Most changes, after all, do not happen in vacuums; they happen in and through relationships.

You might write down the major changes of your life first. After this, you may more easily see the religious background or connections. Once you acknowledge changes, you can more easily identify your greatest change which you can write about in this exercise.

AREA 6. FAITH HELPS
As you look back on your life, what areas or elements of the Catholic faith have been most helpful to you—both in good times and in personal trials. (Consider the sacraments, Catholic friends, the mass, etc.)

Background Information
This question asks you to put your experience of change into the larger context of the faith community. What symbols of the Christian community have played a role in shaping your personal religious story?

This area helps to avoid the impression that religious experience is entirely private or secret. By the time someone has gotten to this part of the exercise, a lot of intense reflection has been going on for some time. This question enables you to "come up for air" from your introspective musings and remembering.

AREA 7. BIBLE IMAGE
Many people find that a verse or an entire story from scripture helps them to make sense of their own experiences of faith. Can you identify a verse or story from scripture that clarifies or enlightens your experience? Write the verse or story below as best as you remember it.

Background Information
We often forget that most Catholics have heard the major parts of the Bible read every three years since 1970 and that, Sunday by Sunday, we have been reciting psalm verses, singing songs with scriptural phrases, and reading banners and bulletins with verses of the scriptures.

Which ones of these have come to form the most ready association for you? Is there a connection between your favorite scripture verse (or story), your image of God, and your religious experiences?

This area invites you to see some of your own experience as part of the scriptural story of the Christian tradition. The connection between scriptural experience and your own experience will put you in tune with the ongoing revelation of God.

AREA 8. FEELINGS
Pause for a moment now and consider the feelings and impressions that the exercise evokes in you regarding your Catholic faith. Summarize these feelings and impressions below.

Background Information
This area provides the occasion to "come down" from the intensely reflective mood that this exercise can create. You now can begin to "abstract" or "pull away from" the experience by having to describe it or define it.

Further, if you have had difficulty with the exercise, this section gives you a reason to say why and not feel inadequate because you had difficulty.

THE SUMMARY SHEET
The summary sheet asks you to reorganize the information and memories you have gathered into a "story." It imagines you talking with an inactive Catholic.

To be sure, this is a somewhat artificial device, but it has an important purpose: to help you put your experiences into a form that you might be able to share with others. Through this kind of device, you can begin to see the story elements in your life as well as the relevance of your experience for helping others in your family, in your ministries and parish involvement, and in your other relationships.

At this point, feel free to delve, prayerfully and openly, into *Discovering My Experience of God.*

Quiet yourself, and ask for the guidance of the Holy Spirit.

WORKSHEET

AREA 1. THE BACKDROP
As you reflect on your life, what are the most important religious dates that you remember? Think about your confirmation, marriage, ordination, religious profession, or other events. On the timeline below, place those dates and events on the top of the line and then, below the line, jot down the key people associated with that experience. These dates form the context for your personal witness.

(Dates and events)

(People)

WORKSHEET

AREA 2. FIRST AWARENESS
Try to remember when you first experienced an awareness of God. Recall the setting, the people present, the particular feelings, how old you were. Write these memories below. Also reflect on whether or not this awareness persisted.

WORKSHEET

AREA 3. POWERFUL MOMENTS
Recall the most powerful religious moments in your life—times of great feeling, awakening, or decisive events. (These can be times of joy as well as sorrow.) What happened? What were your feelings? What images of God did they give you? What images of other people?

WORKSHEET

AREA 4. IMAGES OF GOD

Describe the predominant images of God in your life right now. Is God a strong father, a consoling mother, a healer, a savior, a providential guide, a . . . ?

WORKSHEET

AREA 5. CHANGE

Look back on your life and identify your greatest change. It may have been during your teen or young adult years, or at the beginning or later points of your marriage, or at the start of a career or vocation. As you think about this change, recall what life was like for you "before" and "after." The areas below will help you to reflect on this experience.

My greatest change:

The ways I perceive myself "before" and "after":

       Before   After

WORKSHEET

What was the role of faith in that change?

Who helped you most during that change? And what was their faith?

26

WORKSHEET

AREA 6. FAITH HELPS

As you look back on your life, what areas or elements of the Catholic faith have been most helpful to you—both in good times and in personal trials. (Consider the sacraments, Catholic friends, the mass, etc.)

WORKSHEET

AREA 7. BIBLE IMAGE

Many people find that a verse or an entire story from scripture helps them to make sense of their own experiences of faith. Can you identify a verse or story from scripture that clarifies or enlightens your experience? Write the verse or story below as best as you remember it.

WORKSHEET

AREA 8. FEELINGS
Pause for a moment now and consider the feelings and impressions that the exercise evokes in you regarding your Catholic faith. Summarize these feelings and impressions below.

SUMMARY SHEET

You are now more aware of key elements that make up your story of faith. Now we invite you to take these ingredients and develop a personal witness that will enable you to enrich others. The framework below provides one way for you to put your story into a convincing and meaningful form.

Imagine yourself talking to a friend who is an inactive Catholic, but who now seems open to reconsidering his or her relationship with the church. How might you witness to this person? Remember that this sharing does not have to sound like a well-rehearsed "presentation," but rather something that you can tell comfortably, always being aware of the sensitivities and needs of the person listening. Create your story by completing each of the following areas.

My Personal Witness
The general facts about my Christian life are rather simple and even uneventful . . .
[*Here present the information in Area 1.*]

SUMMARY SHEET

Yet along with these events in my Christian life, other events
have led me to a new awareness of God. For example I
remember . . .
[*Here present the information in Area 2.*]

And some moments were even quite powerful . . .
[*Here present the information in Area 3.*]

SUMMARY SHEET

These experiences are important because they helped me to know God. In fact, I have come to see God as . . .
[*Here present the information in Area 4.*]

I also am aware of God's care during a great change in my life. One change I remember is . . . And I know this change wouldn't have happened without God's presence.
[*Here present the information in Area 5.*]

32

SUMMARY SHEET

As I look back I can honestly say that the Catholic faith has enriched my life. True, I have had my failings and I have doubted at times, but I know that my faith has made me a better person. What I like best about the Catholic Church is . . .
[*Here present the information in Area 6.*]

Sometimes a verse or story from the Bible sums up my religious feelings. One that really speaks to me is . . .
[*Here present the information in Area 7.*]

SUMMARY SHEET

When I take the time to think about the gift of my Catholic faith,
I feel . . .
[*Here present the information in Area 8.*]

I know that God really cares for me and that God cares for all
people. That is why I am happy to share my "faith story" and
hope that my sharing will help you discover God's presence in
your life.

34

Part II

The remaining three chapters of this book are designed to help put this exercise into context.

In Chapter 3, we offer some things for your immediate consideration after you've finished this exercise.

In Chapter 4 we present the theological and spiritual assumptions that lie behind *Discovering My Experience of God*. These will invite further reflection on the meaning of your experience.

And in Chapter 5 we give many ideas and suggestions for using this exercise in a variety of pastoral settings for groups seeking spiritual enrichment or training.

3. NOW THAT YOU'VE COMPLETED THE EXERCISE

So, how do you feel? Now that you've completed *Discovering My Experience of God,* what's your basic feeling?

Perhaps it's one of awe, being lost in the multiple details of your own life, those little elements that compose the alphabet of the story of our lives. Or even fear, given the direction that your life may have taken, the avenues not pursued, the moments buried through forgetfulness. Or simple exhaustion at having tried to look squarely at your life from a spiritual point of view. Or, hopefully, joy at the marvels God has worked in you in ways subtle and stark.

Whatever the emotion primarily generated in you as you complete this exercise, let yourself feel it freely because it, too, is part of your experience and part of the task that now lies ahead. Having put words onto these experiences that compose a life, what should happen now? What do you do with the story of your life which has emerged, perhaps for the first time?

Through reflection, action and review, your faith story can become a valuable gem for you and others to treasure as the facets of your life are touched by the light of your reflections and as the jewel of your life story is polished further. None of this has to happen all at once, but it will begin to happen unavoidably soon after you've completed the exercise. The following pages will help you to know what next steps make sense for you.

REFLECTION

Whatever the primary emotion the exercise produces in those who complete it, there is likely to be an atmosphere of great intensity. You may never have sat down and tried to think of your life as a whole, probed memories of God and spiritual experience, sought for your dominant image of God or key scriptural verse nor tried to specify, in this context, the changes your life has undergone.

So, naturally, it's a lot of work. Even if you've given yourself a very leisurely amount of time to complete *Discovering My Experience of God*, it will probably not diminish this feeling of intensity. Two immediate responses to this intensity involve prayer and perspective.

Prayer

The first possibility in your subsequent reflections is prayer: to address the intensity and the basic emotion by bringing them to God. Our feelings can be given over to God, simply for what they are, with a deep sense of gratitude for the mystery that is our own experience—which we now see more clearly as also an experience of God. Surely none of the events we've remembered nor changes we've isolated in ourselves had to be, or had to be the way they were. Surely, too, our lives could have been shaped one way or another at many points, we imagine, with greater or poorer outcomes. But our lives are as they are, showerings of God's creative and redemptive power. Our response may be one of gratitude. "I praise you, Father," Jesus often uttered in his life (e.g. Lk 10:21). "We praise and thank you, God," we utter as a people every time the eucharist is celebrated. So our thanks can be the beginning of prayer now that we've completed the exercise. Moreover, these moments of prayer can help us begin to put our feelings into perspective.

Perspective

A second element of the "reflection" phase can be a different kind of thinking. Now that you have done the work of recalling your spiritual experiences and putting those experiences in words, you can muse over them with a greater flexibility and a longer perspective.

Once we have sketched out an initial view of our personal experience with God, we can begin to notice things about it and look at it from various angles. Instead of the intense remembering involved in developing our religious story, this is a different kind of thinking about our lives: acknowledging surprises and noticing patterns.

A little time spent dealing with the questions below can help get this different kind of thinking underway.

(1) As I look at the spiritual story of my life, what surprises me most? What is the source of the surprise? What can it teach me about myself?

(2) Were there people who seem to run regularly through my story? Who were these people—relatives or friends, or religious figures? Was there a kind of help they always seemed to provide?

(3) What about the special places of my life? Do I think of these as geographical areas (cities, regions of the country) or as more personal spaces (houses I've lived in, churches or vacation places)? Is there a place which always seems to restore me spiritually?

(4) What was the hardest area of my life to put into words? Why was it so hard? Did trying to deal with it through this exercise make it easier?

(5) What were the times of greatest spiritual activity in my life? How do these times relate to my other years, those seemingly less active?

(6) How would I estimate the impact of my belonging to a church? Do I see connections between the exterior events in my life within the church and the internal stages of growth and change?

Give yourself time to muse through these and other questions that occur to you about your personal experience of God right after you finish the exercise and return to them sometime later.

The insights we get into the patterns and surprises of our own experience can be very helpful in making us more sensitive to the kinds of things that are happening in the lives of other people.

ACTION

Unless this exercise is one of pure introspection, it should be raising questions in us such as: What am I supposed to do with my spiritual story? And can my experiences be helpful to others?

One of the purposes of uncovering our experience of God is to equip us to share our faith with others. If completing this exercise has borne any fruit for us, it has at least helped us know that we have spiritual experiences that are precious, that we can express these experiences in words, and that we can shape these words into a story. We can say: This is part of what I know about my life from the point of view of faith and God.

But this remains only introspection unless we learn to be more comfortable about sharing our experience of God with others. Our Catholic heritage has been one marked by quiet, personal devotion. Our natural tendency is, perhaps, to be shy about our beliefs and experiences. The result can be "invisible Catholics" —those who have rich spiritual experiences inside, but never proclaim this new life in Christ other than by the silent witness of a good life. This might well be a time for us to determine that we can be less "invisible" about our faith experience and look for ways to share these experiences appropriately with others.

Certainly, inappropriate sharing can be an embarrassment to others and, ultimately, to ourselves. No one wants to be assaulted by our stories; moreover, there are times when it is simply not appropriate to bring up our faith or open a conversation about religious experiences with others.

One way to test the appropriateness of our sharing is to ask these questions: Who is being helped by my sharing? Do I share for my own satisfaction or because it meets the needs of another? Or, again, is my talking about my faith a gift of charity or is it a form of manipulation? Or, does my sharing put people on the spot or is it making them freer to explore God's role in their lives?

With some reflection and skills, we can make our faith experiences available to others in a way that will truly enrich them. Consider what it would mean to share your faith in these following situations . . .

With a Family Member or a Close Friend

It might be best to think first of a family member or close friend with whom you can share the fruits of this exercise. For married people, a spouse might be ideal; or, for others, a friend with whom one shares a lot would be suitable. It makes no difference if you rarely share "spiritual things" with your spouse or friend. Your experience of completing this exercise gives you a new opportunity to talk about these aspects of your life.

Of course, we are not out to barrage people. The worst thing would be to jump in front of people, wave your completed exercise, and say: "I want to tell you about how I experienced God in my life!" One is not likely to get a pleasing reception with this approach.

However, it is possible to say casually, while informally sharing things, "I'd like to tell you about something I did today. Do you have a few moments?" Then, in your own words, begin with a description of going through the exercise and gradually move from there to something like: "And this is what I learned about myself and my faith."

This kind of sharing with someone close can help build your confidence. Remember that when Jesus sent his disciples to visit in towns, he advised them to find people of "peace" (Lk 10:5). Another way of understanding this wise advice is that we are not called to address first those most distant or hostile to our faith. We begin with those who are "peaceable" and those who are "nearest" to us spiritually.

With a Broader Circle of Friends

This brings us to a natural extension in our sharing: once we become more comfortable with our stories, we are better equipped to share with people less intimately connected with us. This could be a group of people at our church (a discussion group, a club or organization) or it might be a circle of friends. Again, the approach can begin descriptively: "I went through an exercise the other day and it helped me learn some things about myself and my faith. Would you like to hear about it?" This might, in fact, be a way to invite friends to go through the exercise themselves.

The challenge in doing this will be different from sharing with a spouse or a close friend. Your experiences, communicated to a wider group, will begin to be a kind of witness to them about their own spiritual experiences. And, through contact with you, they will begin to think about the importance of your faith (and maybe your church) and what values that might have for them. Once again, the greatest asset you have is your own spiritual experience which no one can take from you and which people can come to admire.

With Acquaintances and Peers
A third occasion for sharing might be in a setting of acquaintances or professional peers: people at work or people with whom you socialize. This, naturally, is a more sensitive situation since religion is not readily spoken about in contemporary society. One does not easily bring up religious topics in these quasi-public settings, and, once the topic is raised, one must be quite sensitive to the feelings of others. People are not open to being "preached at" or being made to feel religiously inferior to another. Nor are people open to engaging in religious controversy. These common rules of etiquette, so to speak, of our secular, pluralistic culture must be kept in mind the more you branch out into public areas with your spiritual story.

That being said, however, religious topics often do arise at work or in social settings. It may be a religious news item, or some scene from a movie or television show, or simply a question a person asks out of curiosity. In these settings, it might be quite appropriate to share your spiritual story as a witness to faith.

One example is an office conversation about religion, when someone might say, "I see the pope gave a speech again. Doesn't he know about the twentieth century and what modern people think? He seems to ask for blind obedience!" In this setting you might contribute to the conversation by opening with a comment like: "Oh, I know people think that Catholics have all these rules, but that's just an impression. I'm a Catholic and I know that my faith has helped me really come to know God. Can I share with you a little about how I feel?" Or, in some situations, it might be better to approach someone later, one-to-one, with an offer to talk about the importance of one's faith experience.

In these situations, the witness to our faith can be tremendous, opening for others the rich spirituality that fills so many Catholic lives. At the same time, our willingness to share means that we are open to hearing and accepting another's spiritual story, even as we expect our experience to be heard and accepted.

REVIEW

Your third direction, once you have finished this exercise, is yet longer-term: reviewing your story occasionally and doing that from different points of view.

Some who have participated in *Discovering My Experience of God* have been able, some six or twelve months later, to go through the exercise again. They are astonished to find that their "personal story has changed." Yet if we think of our lives and the different threads in it, it may well be that our story deepens or that certain facets become more important the more we think about them or appreciate their role in our lives.

Consider completing the exercise again in a few months and comparing your second set of responses with your first. Some of the dominant themes you have discovered will undoubtedly be present each time you go through the exercise, but the understanding you have of God's role in your life may well deepen through periodic use of the exercise.

Another way to review your story is from different perspectives. For example, you might think about your life by looking at the relationships you have formed over the years. Who has been influential? How? When? Why? And how do these relationships reveal the face of God? As another example, you might look at your life intellectually, evolving a story of faith from the kinds of questions you asked through the decades of your life. Or you might look at the ways you have prayed throughout the years as a way to manifest your ongoing story of faith.

Now that you have completed this exercise, some of the more challenging and interesting occasions lie in front of you. You can approach them with the assurance that God, who has been present to you all your years, will continue to be present, guiding and supporting you. The next chapter, "Understanding Your Experience," will help you to reflect on your own faith story from yet another angle: the theological and spiritual assumptions that lie behind *Discovering My Experience of God*.

4. UNDERSTANDING YOUR EXPERIENCE

Now that you have spent some time writing and reflecting about your experience of God, we invite you to deepen your understanding by considering the assumptions on which this exercise is based.

ASSUMPTIONS
The assumptions on which we have built *Discovering My Experience of God* flow from the heart of Catholic life and faith. Understanding these assumptions will help you to affirm the rich value of your faith.

Assumption #1: Religious Experience Is Usual
People do have religious experience, and that experience is important. The more we imagine the realm of the spiritual as unusual, exclusive or strange, the fewer people seem to have access to it.

Yet people concern themselves about God, right living, prayer, personal struggles, moral choices and human justice almost every day of their lives. All of this is religious experience. If someone decides that he or she will give two hours a week to help feed the poor as a sign of God's care, this person is motivated by spiritual meaning. Another person may find that same intensity of meaning from reading the scriptures or from attending a prayer group. Still another person may find the most powerful religious associations through the beauty of creation. All are valid spiritual experiences which form one's personal faith.

A highly professional man—a news reporter connected to a major TV station—was puzzled when he was completing *Discovering My Experience of God*. "I can't separate in my mind what is a 'religious experience' from one that isn't," he complained. This is the exact point: why should you even try?

Certainly we know some experiences are sinful; we cringe

from them even as we remember them. But among all of life's other experiences, cannot God be present? Cannot God be guiding us, shaping our histories as they unfold? Some of these experiences have an explicit religious setting because they happen in church or are connected with special moments of prayer. But many of these experiences are simply that—experiences of life. God is also present there.

Assumption #2: Conversion Is Ongoing

Discovering My Experience of God assumes that conversion happens throughout one's life. While there may be moments of great breakthrough, when "scales fall from our eyes" as they did for St. Paul, there are developments between these great moments that merit consideration as well.

Perhaps a person has two or three central decisions to make in life. Are not these decisions ratified or disqualified in the subsequent steps that either implement or undermine the basic decision? Experiencing "conversion" does not end the process; instead, it starts a more profound process.

"Have you been saved?" has become a famous question! Not only have many of us felt uneasy when people have asked us this, but the question has become an almost comical caricature of a certain style of evangelical piety.

Yet why are we uneasy? Because we think we haven't been saved? Or because we think that salvation is not a relevant concept? Or because we think that salvation is not able to be known?

Perhaps the reason is that this question assumes there is one point of salvation in a life—a decisive moment of conversion and change—and this doesn't correspond to our experience. We've never doubted God's salvation in our lives; it's just that we keep trying to reaffirm the reality of that grace again and again.

Gail Sheehy created a new set of images for people in her famous book *Passages* (New York: Dutton, 1976). There she constructed a vision of life as a set of thresholds through which people must pass if they will mature through life.

This may be a fairer image of life. To be sure, there are decisive thresholds. Coming to take our faith absolutely seriously is one of them. But every threshold opens up yet another one, in the future, as the image of Christ is progressively formed in us.

Assumption #3: Conversion Happens on Many Levels
We imagine conversion as the anguished conclusion to a great search, and sometimes it is that. More often, however, it is an invitation to further growth and change which happens on various levels in people's experience.

Conversion to Jesus is central in Christian life, but does that conversion stand in isolation from other changes? Conversion to Jesus takes place within a set of changes that affect not only "who I am" but "whom I belong to"—the community with which I identify. Thus, when someone starts involving himself or herself with a new group of people, that may well be conversion.

Or when someone undertakes a moral commitment or a change of behavior, that may be conversion. In fact, some of this change might happen even before an explicit conversion to Jesus.

Conversion might show itself in daily perseverance in spite of doubts or questions; it might show itself in generosity to the poor or generosity with one's talents. Conversion might be revealed in pursuing deep questions or undertaking another form of prayer. Conversion, which is the work of God's grace, might even happen to us long before we have realized it!

One young man has struggled through life all his years. In and out of foster care, in and out of family court, in and out of school and, naturally, in and out of criminal court, his life would not be judged successful by many. In such a life, a radical turn from crime to Christian living would look like a miracle. And he has certainly been invited to such a change! Yet in such a life as this, even to change from despair, even to renounce his own image of needing to fail, would be miraculous—and would be the beginning of conversion.

Our being healed spiritually hints at other healings that must take place. Our being healed in other areas of our lives reveals the spiritual healing God is always offering us.

Assumption #4: Religious Experience Is Nestled Within Our Relationships

This exercise assumes that religious experience is not isolated from the others who make up the fabric of our lives: those we have committed ourselves to, those who have accompanied us on our journey in life, those who have been present to us in need, and those whom we have helped. Our religious experience is wrapped up in our work, our family life, our sport and recreation. It is part of any wholesome change we undergo.

As an example, look for a moment at the idea of "church." Perhaps thirty years ago, this word would have evoked in us an image of St. Peter's in Rome or an image of St. Anthony's down the street. Now, more than three decades into the reforms of the Second Vatican Council, this image is likely to evoke in us an image of people—family members, people in service at the parish church, elderly people or children we have ministered to, or others who have touched us.

What a transformation! From stones to the "living stones" that scripture talks about in 1 Peter 2:5—the people who form the communities of our worship.

"Faith," "church" and other such words now represent for us the *association* of people, the *community* of others who form the network of my faith experience. It is in just such associations, in community, in relationships with others, that the heart of my life exists. Likewise with faith.

To see the connectedness of religious experience with so many relationships that form our lives helps us have the courage to share our own faith stories. We can begin to point out, in a very simple and human manner, the ways in which faith is latent in our experiences with other people. Even more, we can begin to see how sharing our faith is really asking other people to begin or deepen relationships with people who believe.

48

Assumption #5: Everyone Can Express Some Part of His or Her Faith

This instrument assumes that people, when given the opportunity, can learn to verbalize their experiences of faith. It may be that verbalization is not the most important thing for faith; it may also be that our experiences lose something when put into words.

Even so, the process of finding words is the process of making human, intelligible and shareable what could seem quite strange or private. When we share our values, we know them better. When we find the words, we have a gift to give to others. When we say our experiences out loud, we have a chance to gain new insights into them.

What is more common than feeling at a loss for words? Often this happens when people join groups that look for spontaneous prayer. One young teenage girl became involved in such a group—a Bible class for high schoolers. Everyone would be invited to pray but this young woman always resisted the invitation. One day, almost by common consent, the group maneuvered her into praying and she was speechless, barely babbling some introduction to the Lord's Prayer. But the group was moved. Even more, she was moved. The next week she raised her hand and volunteered to lead the prayer, showing a comfort and an ability to articulate that surprised all present—but no one more than she! After a while she became a master of spontaneous prayer.

Was this ability suddenly gained? Most likely, she had the ability to pray spontaneously but, layering so many false images of what she thought was expected before her eyes, she was blocked. Only when she began to see that it was possible and easy to pray (because no one was expecting elaborate orations from her) was she able to pray freely.

This would be equally true about the even more threatening idea of sharing our faith. We have so many layered images of what might be expected of us and so many insecurities about the depth of our own faith experience that we naturally clam up.

The exercise in this booklet demonstrates that every one of us has authentic religious experience and that very little is asked of us except to put that experience into our own words and say them to others at appropriate moments. As the young teenager discovered, it's not only possible: it may be easier than we ever imagined!

Our faith, in fact, becomes more secure the more freely we learn to express and explain it. Like so many things in life, we don't feel we know something until we can put it into words that others can grasp. Everyone who has taught children can testify to this truth.

This exercise assumes that people have faith experiences and they can come to put those experiences into words. It also assumes that doing this can be the beginning of learning to share those experiences with another. Finally, it assumes that every believer can develop skills in this area.

SOME CONCLUDING THOUGHTS

Now that you have finished the exercise and reflected on your faith experience, consider for a moment the great value of your faith. Remember, one thing no one can take from you is your experience—experience that has been touched, again and again, by God, experience rich in love, faith and hope.

The realization of your religious story, that personal faith story that is uniquely yours, can motivate your prayer, giving you yet more reasons to glorify God. And it can motivate your apostolic sense, giving you more confidence in your ability to bring a word of faith to others.

Just as you might have doubted whether you could do this exercise, you might now be doubting about whether you can share what you know about your own life of faith. Yet you have every reason not to fret or doubt. You know God has touched you!

You now might be more inclined to help others discover their experience of God. You can do this easily by providing a setting for them to complete this spiritual exercise. You might invite your family members, friends or neighbors to experience what you have experienced.

This is how the good news has always been spread—by one person telling another.

Now you know you have something to tell!

5. TIPS FOR THOSE ADMINISTERING THE INSTRUMENT

This chapter is designed to assist those who administer *Discovering My Experience of God* to others. We present some examples of its uses which derive primarily from the double-faceted quality of this instrument: inward reflection and outward witness. We present one setting for using this tool on a retreat and a different setting for using this tool in evangelization training. Finally, by way of example, we show the ways in which this pastoral tool can be used to develop and enhance the ministries of the RCIA.

PRELIMINARY CONSIDERATIONS
Regardless of the setting in which you use this instrument, you should consider two questions: What are the needs of the different types of people who will be part of the exercise? And what materials do you need to administer the instrument effectively?

"People" Factors
Because this instrument invites people into rather intense consideration of their memories and experiences, certain unusually extroverted people may have difficulty with it. Trying to find words for such close and sometimes elusive memories simply is too burdensome for them. This difficulty, however, does not arise often. Less than one in a hundred of those who pioneered the exercise were unable to go through it completely.

What happens if someone simply cannot do the exercise? He or she might be directed to the more concrete areas (e.g. asking for the events of one's life, or a favorite scripture passage) and then be encouraged to write a meditation based on that.

Yet another kind of person may have difficulty with this instrument: one who has developed, in another setting, an elaborate witness story. Some people with Pentecostal or charismatic backgrounds may have already learned to verbalize their religious experience in story and witness, and may express impatience with the structure and format of this exercise.

Actually, these people, in spite of their initial feelings, do benefit from *Discovering My Experience of God*. Sometimes witness stories are developed in prayer groups that use a particular kind of language and format. Scriptural verses may be assigned beforehand and various points memorized even before a person's experience is addressed. This instrument can help people review their experience in a fresh way.

Even more tellingly, some people have put their witness story into a kind of "package" that is not readily portable to other settings or readily hearable by other people. The persons with whom they speak may identify them as "too pious" or "too holy roller" even before they hear the message. Instead of the story being a public kind of language that reaches others, it may appear as a strange kind of vocabulary that frightens people away.

The focus on ordinary experience, given in the general format of *Discovering My Experience of God,* encourages people to develop a story that is more serviceable because it has less religious jargon and because it springs from more readily shared experiences in a person's life.

Even people who have developed an elaborate witness story should be encouraged to undertake this exercise. If nothing else, it will at least help them to reflect further on their religious experience.

Material Needed
No matter what setting is used, people will need certain things to use this instrument well. One who administers *Discovering My Experience of God* can go a long way toward making this a rewarding experience for people by taking care of these needs.

(1) Space
People will be writing for at least an hour and a half. They should not be cramped into a small space where they are dodging the

elbows of their co-participants. They will appreciate the sense that people are not looking over their shoulders.

(2) Tables
It would not be wise to administer this exercise in a room filled with sofas or lounge chairs. Even if people have clipboards, this is an uncomfortable setting for extended writing. Make sure that there are tables suitable for writing.

(3) Quiet
People get so deeply involved in the exercise that noise will be a great hindrance, especially as they move beyond Area 2. While people using this tool usually will be quiet, noise may come from outside the room. This should be anticipated and addressed beforehand. You also could remind the participants that, as a courtesy to each other, they should observe silence until every person has completed the exercise.

(4) A Separate Room
Some people will go through the exercise more quickly than others. Rather than have them sitting idle at the table while others are working, or beginning to distract those who are still working, they might be invited to a separate room where coffee, tea and other beverages are available. They can lounge and reflect in this area without disturbing those who are still writing.

(5) Pens
Not everyone carries a pen or pencil. Make sure plenty are available. This exercise cannot be done by two people using the same pen, or by a pen that is running out of ink.

(6) Lighting
Different lighting can, of course, be utilized depending on the settings (i.e. a softer retreat setting or a brighter workshop set-

ting) but it should always be sufficient, whatever the setting, for people to write comfortably for the required amount of time.

(7) A Bible
People will want to consult a Bible, particularly in looking for their favorite scriptural verse or story. Try to have several Bibles available. If anyone knows the Bible well, he or she can be a resource in helping people locate stories that they remember.

ADMINISTERING THE EXERCISE
Before beginning, the administrator must announce clearly that the material written belongs to the participants, is confidential, will not be collected or reviewed by anyone, and will be shared only at their discretion. In fact, the exercise will not tend to develop much "confessional" material, but people need to be reassured in order to be comfortable with exploring their faith experience. If people are uncomfortable, their memories and associations will be, in part, blocked.

The way *Discovering My Experience of God* is actually administered depends on a number of factors. However, the most significant factor is the level of those who are participating. Some will have a facility with writing, verbalizing, and reflecting religiously, while others will have recently come to reflect on their lives in spiritual terms. Some will have been on many retreats and workshops and others will be on their first one. In general, the less experienced the participants, the more the exercise should be done step by step, as a group.

We suggest starting with a general orientation to the exercise and then reading aloud Areas 1 and 2 to the group. Give examples for the time line of Area 1 and talk about the kind of information sought in Area 2.

With less experienced groups, or in retreat settings, it might make sense to go through all eight areas—area by area—giving the group time to reflect on each one. This includes the entire group beginning the Summary Sheet at the same time.

Since so much depends on the setting, we present some of the possibilities of administering this exercise in various settings.

SETTINGS IN WHICH TO USE *DISCOVERING MY EXPERIENCE OF GOD*

The simplicity of this tool invites its use in many kinds of settings: young adult retreats, evangelization team training, confirmation preparation, parent baptismal preparation, religious education teacher training, and small group training.

Basically, the one who gives the exercise must decide if the focus is more reflective of personal development (such as retreats, sacramental preparation, encounter weekend follow-up) or a more extroverted objective of building skills (evangelization or religious education training). For the former, the considerations under the "retreat setting" will be helpful; for the latter, read carefully the section under "training sessions."

THE RETREAT SETTING

The quiet reflection that is part of *Discovering My Experience of God* serves a retreat setting very well. This instrument can even form the major substance of a retreat experience. However, people need to be challenged after reviewing the memories of their lives, and the ideal retreat setting would involve using this instrument in conjunction with more extroverted, sharing kinds of activities.

In a retreat setting, people do not need to stay in the same room while writing. The quietness and reflective qualities sought in retreats may be best served by inviting people to move around to different parts of the room or building where the retreat is taking place.

The time given for the exercise in a retreat should also be more flexibly conceived. People might be invited to take a longer period of time filling out the eight areas and the summary sheets. You could suggest that they visit the chapel, talk with the retreat director, or read scriptures when writing and reflecting.

Depending on the time people want to put into this, an entire morning might be devoted to filling out the eight areas, with the summary sheets being done at another time (perhaps even another day) to give people time to absorb their memories.

However long people have to complete the exercise, encourage them to talk about it, put it into context, and relieve some of the intensity resulting from their thinking and writing. The best format for doing this is through small groups (with never more than eight in a group!) in which each participant has the opportunity to speak. While people need enough time to discuss, the time should be limited and specified. This will help circumvent any desire to "overtalk" the experience.

Here are some questions that we have used effectively for the small group discussions in retreat settings:

1. How did you feel during the exercise?

2. In what ways do you think others would benefit from an exercise like this?

3. What are the most obvious patterns that you observed through doing this exercise?

4. Name one way that God seems to have been present in your life.

5. How would you imagine your future life after having reviewed the past?

6. What is there about your faith that you would want to share with someone else?

The questions that are developed should be more general at first and ask for descriptive answers that everyone can readily share. You can ask questions requiring greater personal revelation more effectively later.

One way in which a retreat experience can be shaped—perhaps with a parish community in mind—might be as follows.

A Retreat Schedule

9:00	**Assemble, coffee, donuts, greeting, registration**
9:30	**Welcome, orientation, opening prayer**
9:35	**Scripture reading**
9:40	**Short talk**
9:50	**Introduction to *Discovering My Experience of God***
10:00	**Completing the eight areas**
11:00	**Completing the summary sheets**
11:30	**Small group discussion**
12:00	**Lunch/break**
1:00	**Scripture reading**
1:10	**Large group discussion**
1:30	**Scriptural reflection (perhaps a dialogue form)**
1:45	**Prayer**
2:00	**Closing**

In choosing scriptures for this kind of retreat, you might select from the more "personal" ones which highlight God's call: the call of Samuel (1 Sam 3:1–18), the call of Matthew (Mt 9:9), Paul's experience (Gal 1:11–24), or Jesus' words from the last supper according to John (Jn 15:1–17).

Teenagers can undertake this exercise with benefit, although they may seem somewhat apprehensive about their lack of experience. For example, they may report that they have not had many great changes in their lives. If the group is composed of young people, it will help to talk about those areas (particularly Area 5), giving examples that will focus less on dramatic changes

(I am a recovering alcoholic) and more on progressive ones (I was always insecure but now I feel comfortable with myself).

People preparing for confirmation will benefit from this exercise not only by sharpening their "awareness" dimension but especially their "witness" dimension. One might want to think of ways to encourage candidates for confirmation to share their stories and experiences so that these sharings seem natural and not forced or manipulated.

A TRAINING SESSION

The training or workshop element brings out very clearly a key purpose for doing the exercise: actually developing a witness story that flows from one's personal experiences as a committed and believing Catholic. *Discovering My Experience of God,* from its very inception, has as its ultimate goal to equip Catholics to acknowledge and share their faith more confidently with others. The more spiritually aware people are of God's work in their lives, the more likely they are to share their faith with others.

The tone for a training session should be quite different from that for a retreat. A retreat basically looks inward while a training session, by definition, looks outward at tasks, goals and skills. People come to these events differently disposed. On a retreat they seek quiet reflection, but at a workshop they want information.

Those who direct workshops must attend to things like time, schedule, and equipment needed. Determine specific times for activities during the workshop and keep the session "rolling." As a general rule, the workshop should allow no more than one hour for completing the eight areas and one half hour for the summary sheets.

People at a workshop should generally do the exercise in the same room. This creates the sense of "work being done" and allows them to see how they are keeping up with others in going through the exercise. In addition, doing the exercise in the same room gives a sense of action and energy which many come to expect at workshops.

The administrator at a workshop might also be more aggressive in encouraging the participants to share their personal stories of faith because that is why the participants have come. In some of the workshops in which this instrument was tested, people were asked, when they finished the exercise, to find one person in the room they did not know before and, if possible, to share their stories. The result was startling: everyone shared and people did not want to stop!

It might be better in a workshop setting not to start immediately with *Discovering My Experience of God* because this exercise tends to dominate a whole training session through drawing people so powerfully inward. Contexted with presentations, discussions and question-and-answer time, it forms a perfect balance for a workshop experience. Another alternative would be to have a series of training sessions, with this exercise as one of the sessions clearly situated among others.

The topics that should be included in a workshop like this are: Catholic evangelization, the nature of witness, the importance of witness, and situations in which one may witness effectively.

A sample workshop training day might be scheduled as follows.

An Evangelization Workshop Schedule

9:00	Registration, coffee, donuts
9:20	Opening prayer
9:30	Presentation: Catholic Evangelization Today
10:15	Break
10:30	Questions
11:00	Presentation: Giving Witness (more informal than the opening talk)
11:30	Discussion
12:00	Lunch/break
12:45	Orientation to *Discovering My Experience of God*
1:00	Fill out the eight areas

2:00	**Fill out the summary sheets**
2:30	**Break**
2:45	**Small group discussion**
3:15	**General discussion/questions**
3:45	**Prayer**
4:00	**Evaluation and closing**

N.B. If people are going to share their stories, they should do this after completing their summary sheets. Give at least twenty minutes extra for this kind of sharing.

Some have found that conducting training sessions on two evenings works better for participants than committing one larger block of time. If this is true in your situation, consider scheduling the events of the morning session, as described above, into one evening and the events of the afternoon session into the second evening.

Questions for discussion should be different from those given at a retreat. Rather than focusing inwardly, they should focus on tasks, goals and skills, thus clarifying and reinforcing the skills people are absorbing through the workshop.

Some sample questions that might serve the purpose of a training session are:

1. What parts of the exercise did you find most difficult?

2. How has this exercise enabled you to think differently about witnessing?

3. In what ways have people witnessed to you? What was your reaction?

4. What areas of your faith do you think others would benefit from hearing about? Why?

5. How can you, as a Catholic, share a distinct witness with other people?

Because *Discovering My Experience of God* involves the participants so intensely, it can serve as an ideal workshop tool, almost ensuring the attention of all the participants. The more it can be woven into other topics about witnessing, evangelization and outreach, the more likely some members will become equipped to share their faith.

MINISTRY TRAINING FOR THE RCIA

The third example which we offer as a model for using *Discovering My Experience of God* is sponsor training within the Rite of Christian Initiation of Adults. Research tells us that the sponsor plays one of the most important roles in the catechumenal ministry. It's a role of befriending, of modeling the ways in which to live the Catholic way of life, of forming bonds with the catechumen or candidate.

By its very nature, the ministry of sponsor is not a "professional" ministry, not one which requires advanced degrees in religious education or theology. Rather, the ideal sponsor is one who is seen by the catechumen or candidate as "one like him" or "one like her," a person who serves as a model of living the ordinary Christian life as part of a parish community.

Discovering My Experience of God can be used effectively in sponsor training sessions precisely because of the unique role of the sponsor. The pastor and parish staff usually select sponsors whom they think will make a good "match" for the catechumen or candidate. Yet many potential sponsors feel inadequate to serve in this ministry. They may say, "I don't know enough about my faith," or "What qualities do I have that will make me a good sponsor?" (which is another way of saying, "Why did you choose me?").

Used as part of a larger sponsor training program, *Discovering My Experience of God* can equip sponsors for their roles in two ways: discovering once again, and even more powerfully, the giftedness of their own spiritual journey, and learning how to share their faith with catechumens or candidates. Sponsors find this training valuable because it enables them to discover the contours of their inner journey which, in turn, gives them more confidence to witness to others.

A sample sponsor training day might look like this.

A RCIA Sponsor Training Schedule

9:00	**Registration, coffee, donuts**
9:20	**Opening prayer**
9:30	**Presentation: The Role of the Sponsor in the RCIA**
10:15	**Break**
10:30	**Questions**
11:00	**Presentation: The Importance of Faith Sharing for Sponsors (perhaps given by experienced sponsors)**
11:30	**Discussion**
12:00	**Lunch/break**
12:45	**Orientation to *Discovering My Experience of God***
1:00	**Fill out the eight areas**
2:00	**Fill out the summary sheets**
2:30	**Break**
2:45	**Group discussion**
3:15	**Practicing giving one's witness (done in pairs)**
3:45	**Large group discussion**
4:00	**Evaluation and closing prayer**

You may find that RCIA ministers in your parish prefer evening sessions to a longer block of time. If this is the case, consider breaking the above schedule into two evening sessions.

The following questions can be used to focus the group discussions.

1. What was the easiest part of completing *Discovering My Experience of God?*

2. What part of your faith do you think would be of real value to share with a catechumen or candidate?

3. What is your greatest fear about sharing your personal witness with the person whom you are sponsoring?

4. Did you find in your personal story of faith someone who exhibited the same qualities of a "sponsor" for you? What difference did that make in your life?

The second year you use *Discovering My Experience of God* as part of your sponsor training, consider asking a sponsor from last year's training session to give a witness to this year's class. The person could share her witness, tell about the situation(s) in which she shared her story with her catechumen, and what effect this sharing had on their relationship.

The sponsor is not the only RCIA minister who could benefit from completing *Discovering My Experience of God.* Those who serve on the RCIA pre-catechumenate team are certainly presented with ample opportunities to share their story. A sensitive personal witness will usually encourage inquirers to feel more comfortable in doing the same. Consider too the possibility of using this pastoral tool to equip the newly baptized or those received into full communion with the church during the season of mystagogia. The neophytes are encouraged to reflect on their experience of faith during this period. Moreover, the Easter season is the time in which the church wants to send these fervent Christians out to witness to their new-found faith. Helping the neophytes to share their story in a training session would do many the valuable service of channeling all their new-found spiritual energy into a sensitive and focused personal witness.

Parish-Wide Potential

We have presented three settings in which using *Discovering My Experience of God* would be of great value. Applying the principles in all three examples, you can see the potential of helping people to share their faith in numerous situations: in families, in the workplace, in civic relationships, as part of the liturgy team's retreat.

Imagine what your parish would be like if all parishioners were equipped to share their personal witness confidently and competently when the occasion presents itself. This would certainly be a marvelous way to share in Christ's mission of bringing the gospel to every person.

ABOUT THE AUTHORS

FRANK DeSIANO, CSP, holds a Doctor of Ministry degree from Boston University. In 1988 he began Parish Based Evangelization, a ministry he directs in the Washington, D.C. area to help parishes develop evangelizing skills and projects. Fr. DeSiano has written numerous articles and several books, including *Searching for Sense: The Logic of Catholic Belief,* and more recently, *Presenting the Catholic Faith: A Modern Catechism for Inquirers* (both published by Paulist Press). He co-directs, with Kenneth Boyack, CSP, The Paulist Evangelization Training Institute.

KENNETH BOYACK, CSP, the director of the Paulist National Catholic Evangelization Association, holds a Doctor of Ministry degree from The Catholic University of America. He also serves as continental director of **Evangelization 2000** in North America. He edited *Catholic Evangelization Today* (Paulist Press, 1986), co-authored *The Catholic Faith Inventory* (Paulist Press, 1987), and served as editor-in-chief for *The Catholic Way of Life* (PNCEA, 1990). He serves as a consultor to the NCB Committee on Evangelization and also serves as coordinator for the development of their National Plan and Strategy for Catholic Evangelization in the United States.